THINGS I'D TELL MY DAUGHTER

PATRICE ROSSI

Copyright © 2025 | Second Edition | Patrice Rossi
All rights reserved.
ISBN 979-8-218-75841-7

DEDICATION

Mom, I love you.
I know you did the best you could with what you had.
I love who I am today, and I've finally accepted you had so much to do with that.
I wish we'd been close.
I wish we could've talked.
About everything.
And most of all, I wish I could say I love you just one more time.

ACKNOWLEDGMENTS

Natalie, you taught me change and growth are always possible, and life can be exactly what I choose to make it.

Caleb, you helped me make peace with my own mother when you told me *"Mom, I love my life the way it is. If you'd been different then I'd be different, and I love who I am. So, it's all good."* I am so honored to be your mom.

Liam, you are an incredibly gifted songwriter and have always been able to put to words what's on your mind, what you're feeling, or what you've done. No matter how big, how scary, how vulnerable that thing might be. You are an inspiration to me and I'm so grateful to be your mom.

Caleb and Liam, you are who I think about every day, who I consider in relation to my future goals and plans, and my most favorite humans. I get to see you change and grow and love as you move through this world. I love you both more than I can ever put to words.

CONTENTS

1. WHY   1
2. YOU   3
3. STUFF   43
4. THE BIG PICTURE   77
5. SEX   89
6. LOVE   105
7. HIM   121

About the Author   139

1

WHY

"A mother can only give her child what she has." Those words resonated deeply within my soul when I first read them. They're taken from *Mother Hunger* written by Kelly McDaniel. I found and devoured this book in a weekend, relating to everything she had to say. From the moment I began reading, I couldn't put it down. Maybe someday you'll read it.

Just before that statement, Kelly writes "When we understand that mothers love us the best way they can and the only way they know how, blame has no place."

I read Kelly's book about halfway into writing this one. I'm writing this book to you, my beautiful daughter, and at the same time I can't help but think of my own mother. And her mother. And her mother's mother. We've all done the best we knew how.

This is why I'm writing this for you. I've forgiven my mother and finally let go of so many resentments I'd held on to; pieces of my life that had become my story. My reasons why. Why did this happen? Why did that happen? Why am I the way I am? Why? Why? Why?

I know that you also have your story, your reasons why.

I'd always dreamt of having a mother who'd been able to talk to me, like truly talk to *me*. All the things I believed a mother should be willing, able and even excited to share with her own daughter.

My mom was not like that. I never had chats about what it was like to fall in love; what to expect the first time I had sex; what to look for in a good man; how to manage my money; things my crazy brain might tell me; and that I am truly okay, no matter what. That I was beautiful, but also smart. That what and who I am on the inside is so much more important than what or who I am on the outside.

I now understand completely. *She could only give me what she had.*

I want to do better with you. I'm ready to see you as the incredible woman you are. To acknowledge your amazingness, your heart, your mind, your body, your soul. Every bit of you that makes you you.

I see you. I have seen you. I've been watching you grow and have felt the tugs at my heart as I feel you reaching for the stars, following your dreams, and hitting speed bumps along the way. I've watched you fall. I've watched you get back up. I've held you while you cried. I've let go of you when you needed space. I've sat in silence when you've hated me, knowing that hate is not the opposite of love. I remember that I've also hated my own mother. Because I loved her so much. You are my daughter. I could not ever have asked for more.

I'm going to tell you all the things. The things I wish my mom had been able to tell me. The juice of life.

2
YOU

JUST THE FACT YOU ARE A LIVING, BREATHING HUMAN IS A MIRACLE. I've never forgotten that.

I can't imagine a world where you don't exist. I have so many hopes and dreams for you. I have my own ideas of how I can see your life, your future. Then I remember that it's not for me to decide. You can be and do anything you put your mind to! What is your heart's desire? What lights your fire? You've always had such an imagination, a creative spirit. Do that. Be that. Or whatever you want. I'll *always* love you.

In the words of E.E. Cummings, "It takes courage to grow up and become who you really are."

That is the truth.

Only be you.

Always.

xo – Mom

"I say if I'm beautiful. I say if I'm strong. You will not determine my story. I will." – Amy Schumer

BE SILLY.

If I could go back to my 20s, silly would be a goal! I took life way too seriously. I didn't play enough.

Let go, be free, look at the silly side of things!

Play. Laugh. Giggle. Roll your eyes. Stick out your tongue. Make funny noises.

Even if you're alone. Sometimes that's the most fun.

Don't take life, or yourself, too seriously.

What's your favorite memory of a time you let yourself be silly? Do you feel free to be silly anytime you want?

BE CURIOUS.

It took me until my late 40s to realize how something as simple as getting curious about things could make so many parts of my life that much better.

Curiosity about feelings was a big one. It was always incredibly easy for my feelings to send me into a spiral. Any sort of feeling that I called 'sad' or 'bad' could ruin my day, my week, my year, my life! At least that's how it would feel. I'm sure you know what I'm talking about.

I started getting curious. *What am I feeling? Why does it feel this way? What does it mean? How do I want to feel? What do I need to do to change how I feel?*

Once I started getting curious, everything got better. I even asked myself random questions.

Why do I own a scale? So, I tossed it. More to come on that one.

Why do I fall in love with men and not women? I just do.

The curiosity is in the asking. Don't be afraid of the answers.

What's something you could get curious about? Is there anything you're afraid to get curious about?

TOSS THE SCALE.

About the scale. I'll never forget the feeling I got when I tossed my perfectly good digital scale into the dumpster. Freedom!! It was incredible. I regret it took me 52 years to figure that one out.

Every morning I'd notice the scale leaning against the wall beside the toilet. And every day. And every night. Really, every time I went into the bathroom! I realized that every single time I saw that damn thing I'd have a thought about my weight. And that thought was most often about the weight *I wasn't*. The weight I thought I *should* be. Uggh! Ridiculous!

Growing up we always had a scale in the bathroom. I thought every woman must have one, to stay healthy! To be conscious of her body! To keep the weight off! *WTF??*

It makes me sad thinking of myself and so many others growing up with that kind of thinking.

Your body is exactly how it should be. If you love your body and treat yourself well, you'll naturally be doing things that keep you healthy.

It's *not* about your weight. Please toss the fucking scale.

What's something you'd be better off tossing? A thing? A belief?

YOU ARE SMART.

Your brains blow me away. Your logic, your knowledge, your talent.

Always keep learning, growing, seeking. It keeps conversations interesting, especially the ones with yourself!

I love it when you tell me things that I don't know. You've been doing that since you were little!

I admire your brilliance, your thought patterns, the way you express yourself.

You are just so smart.

Do you believe you are smart? What's something you know that makes you feel smart?

Be bold.

Speak up. Do that thing. It doesn't matter who's watching, or who isn't. Do it for you. Do it for someone you love.

Take that chance.

Quit that job.

Go after that job.

Start that business.

Ask that question.

Say that thing.

Don't ever let anyone keep you small.

The ones who matter will support your dreams and goals, always.

What's something you want to do that scares you? What's something you've already done that required you to be bad-ass-bold?

YOU ARE BEAUTIFUL.

Your body, mind, heart and soul are precious. You are a beautiful woman, inside and out. Enjoy your physical beauty, embrace it, and don't take it for granted.

Use good sunscreen.
Believe in others.
Wear hats.
Be spiritual.
Wear sunglasses.
Read good books.
Eat good food.
Don't drink too much.
Unless it's water.
Learn new skills.
Get enough sleep.
Exercise.
Be kind, always.
Wash your face before bed.

Always remember that when you are happy you will also be beautiful.

Do you know just how beautiful you are? Do you feel beautiful inside?

Be outrageous.

I always cared too much about what everyone thought. About me. I figured they were all watching every move I made. Judging me. Waiting for me to do that thing, to fail, to fall, so they could laugh.

It kept me small, and it wasn't until I was in my 40s that I learned how to begin to change that. I'm still a work in progress there.

Wear that thing.

Do that thing.

Be that thing.

Say that thing.

Because you can.

People are thinking of you way less than you think they are.

People who are judging are not the ones that matter.

What's one thing you'd do today if you didn't care what anyone thought? What's something outrageous you've already done?

It's not all about you.

I wish it was all about you, because I think you're worth it. But I'm just your mom and I don't get to call the shots.

It's *not* all about you.

That's the good news and the bad news.

When I figured this out, it was seriously life changing. Talk about freedom.

Not only was no one really thinking about me all the time, but also no one needed *me* to think about *them* all the time.

You're just not that important to keeping life moving, to keeping the world turning, which means you have both the time and freedom to do *you*.

And that, my love, is amazing.

Have you felt responsible for someone who isn't your responsibility? How have you let what others might think affect your life?

BE ANYTHING YOU WANT.

It's a wonderful thing when your life's work inspires you to be the best version of you, pays the bills, and maybe even inspires others. I hope you always love the work you do.

If you wake up one day and realize you're no longer inspired or passionate about what you do every day, take a good hard look at what it is you're doing.

Why you're doing it.

What you'd rather be doing.

Then change what you're doing.

That might mean chucking your job, going against the grain, taking classes, taking a gap year, ending a relationship, starting a relationship, being single, doing something that even your closest friends don't understand.

I will always understand and be your biggest fan.

Please be anything you want.

Always.

Is there something that popped into your head when you read this? Something you'd love to do but have never done?

CHECK YOUR MOTIVES.

We all have those parts of us that sometimes tell us things we don't want to hear. Our intuition. Our conscience.

Sometimes I don't want to hear what they might have to say about why I'm doing what I'm doing. Or why I really want to do that thing.

My motives. Am I trying to manipulate a situation? A person? Am I doing that thing so that I can get what I want?

I used to do my best to ignore those messages.

Everything we do has a motive.

I'm working on mine and hoping they're mostly good. It's not always easy. Definitely a work in progress.

I know that when I'm honest with myself about my motives, it makes it easier to do the right thing. The right thing by others.

I spent so much of my life trying to manipulate things into what I wanted them to be. That never works. Not in the long run.

Anyway, just learn to check your motives. You'll be so much happier, you'll sleep better, and you'll have better relationships.

Has checking your motives ever changed your behavior? Is there anything you're doing now that you know is manipulative?

Wear bras and panties that make you feel beautiful.

Toss the ugly bras and panties! Ban the granny panties. No rips, no tears, nothing stretched out, too tight, or ugly.

Who says we have to wear old panties on our period? In fact, maybe that's when we need the most help to feel good about ourselves.

You *always* deserve to feel beautiful and feminine.

Ugly bras and panties *are not* inspiring.

Wear pretty things against your skin, always.

They don't have to be expensive.

They don't have to match.

They should always be beautiful.

Not for him.

Not for them.

For you.

Are you on your way to toss some bras and panties in the trash? What kind of panties make you feel the most beautiful?

EMBRACE IMPERFECTIONS.

Your flaws and imperfections are what make you you. They are what make you human.

Trying to hide imperfections is so much work. It'll make you feel like a fraud. Have you ever had the thought *'if they only knew the real me, then they would (insert hurtful thought here)'*?

We all have those thoughts. Women are so susceptible to imposter syndrome. It's a thing.

Social media is everywhere which makes it difficult to not compare ourselves with other women. Women who seem to be doing it all, having it all, knowing it all. They really *aren't* and they really *don't*. I promise.

We all have imperfections.

If you embrace and own your imperfections, you'll be more loved, more approachable, more relatable.

You'll be so much happier.

I promise.

What's your favorite imperfection? Can you look at your imperfections and consider them quirky, or charming?

It's none of your business what anyone thinks of you.

I wasted so much of my life caring what people thought. It was exhausting. Come to find out, no one was really thinking of me. Not like I thought they were.

No one is thinking of you nearly as much as *you* think of *you*! I promise. Well, except me of course.

Some *will* judge.

Some *will* be jealous.

Some *will* be waiting for failure.

Some *will* talk behind your back.

The ones who do those things are *not* the ones who matter!

So, it's none of your business what they think.

About you, or anything really.

Is worrying about what people might think holding you back from doing something? What's one thing you'd do if absolutely no one's opinion mattered?

FEELINGS ARE NOT FACTS.

The ones that make you feel amazing. The ones that make you wish you were dead. They can change in an instant. The only guarantee about feelings is that they *will* change.

Have you ever been sitting and thinking about how amazing things are, and then suddenly you get a random thought that sends those amazing feelings spinning? Literally nothing in your world changed, but your feelings did a complete 180.

Please remember that.

Especially when your heart is breaking, when your sadness seems overwhelming, but also when you are in ecstatic moments, having the time of your life, when it seems nothing could get any better.

Those feelings will change too. And that's ok.

You're ok.

Can you remember a time you experienced a massive shift in a feeling for no apparent reason? Do you have moments where you feel like nothing will ever be ok again? Or, that nothing could ever go wrong?

FIND SOMEONE YOU CAN TELL YOUR SECRETS TO.

When I got sober I learned something life-changing.

You are only as sick as your secrets.

I grew up with secrets. And as an adult, I had secrets. Not the good kind. Not the sweet secrets a close friend would tell me after swearing me to secrecy. I'm talking about my own secrets. The kind that fester and grow and then affect my life and my relationships, and my self-esteem.

Please find someone you can tell your darkest secrets to. We all have them. But it's what we do with them that makes all the difference. The difference between unsettled and content. The difference between good sleep and bad. The difference between a healthy body, mind, heart and soul and an afflicted spirit.

The bad secrets will eat at you. They will undermine relationships, goals, dreams, and life.

Please find that someone.

Who's that person you can tell your deepest darkest secrets to? Are you holding on to a secret today that you know is better shared with someone you trust?

You hold the answers.

Your body is wise beyond its years.

Your body knows what you need and will give you clues, if not the whole answer, if you let it.

Get to know your body, your soul, your intuition.

We, as women, tend to not listen. It's easier to give people and things the benefit of the doubt. It doesn't matter if it's about that friend, that man, that job, anything.

If you learn to recognize and then *listen to* your intuition, you'll often be absolutely 100% right...for you.

If you're like me, you won't always listen. But still, your body does hold all the answers.

Do you listen to your intuition? Is there anything niggling at you today that you just 'know' isn't ok?

OWN YOUR BODY.

Own it! Fully, completely 100% own it. Your curves, your lines, your quirks, your flaws. Every single part.

My body has been a lot of different things, shapes and sizes, different levels of fit. All the things. I haven't always loved it, let alone owned it.

I've learned to love and embrace my body, no matter what, but it's taken a ridiculously long time. I hope you get to that place faster than I did.

Stand in front of a mirror. Naked. Look yourself in the eye, then look at your body. Hug yourself. Caress your body gently with love. Your hips. Your belly. Your butt. Your neck. Your scars. Even your toes. Appreciate where it's taken you. What it's given you. The things it's felt. The things it's survived. The way it works for you, every single day.

What's your favorite thing about your body? Can you say I love you out loud when you're in front of the mirror, naked?

SHOW UP.

Show up for everything and everyone important to you.

Most of all, show up *for yourself*.

Have you made a commitment to yourself? Show up for it.

Have you made a commitment to someone else? Show up for it.

Even when you don't want to. Especially when you don't want to.

If you realize that something no longer serves you, then address it. If you no longer want to show up for something or someone, have that conversation.

But until you do, keep showing up.

That's character. That's integrity.

How you show up for yourself is how you show up for life.

Keep your promises.

Honor your commitments.

Do you show up for yourself? Is there anything you've not shown up for without having that important conversation first?

Just. Be.

I was about 52 years old before I could truly say that I enjoyed just being with me. That I could look forward to those times when I knew I was going to be alone.

No plans, no schedule, no distractions.

Learning to Just Be has probably been the single most defining ability that has helped me grow and change in so many other ways.

It blows my mind how often I realize I prefer my time spent with just me over spending it with others or doing those things that used to keep me from having to be with myself.

If you're already able to be your own best company, that's truly something to be proud of. At least as far as I'm concerned.

It took so much work for me to get to that place. It was hands-down the best, and most difficult, work I've ever done. A lot of clearing out, cleaning out, getting curious, why I'd always had the need, or better yet the compulsion, to keep myself busy, distracted.

Do the work.

Whatever it takes.

To learn to Just Be.

Do you love the time you get to spend with just yourself? Do you know the difference between being alone and being lonely?

3
STUFF

STUFF. I love random words. You already know that. To me stuff is the perfect word to describe things that are just the way they are. They might be able to fit here, there, or anywhere, or I just felt like putting them where I did for no particular reason.

Those are the things you'll find here.

xo – Mom

"Life is too short to stuff a mushroom." – Shirley Conran

DO THAT THING.

Whatever *it* is. Do it.

I'm a firm believer that our biggest regrets will be the things we didn't do.

It doesn't matter if you do it and fail. Unless of course it's jumping out of an airplane. We don't want that to fail.

Start that business.

Take that trip.

Buy that thing.

Say I love you to that person.

Quit that job.

Take that job.

Whatever it is that's burning in your heart, sort it out and then do it.

Sometimes you will fail.

Sometimes you will fall.

You'll get back up.

You'll be ok.

In fact, you'll be even better for it.

I promise.

I will always be there for you.

What are all those things you so badly want to do? What are some of those things you've already done?

PAY YOURSELF FIRST.

Always pay yourself first. When you get that paycheck. When you start that business. Even when you have bills to pay. It doesn't matter what your situation is, *always* pay yourself first.

However you do it, it comes down to telling your money where to go and when. If you don't it will go places without you. Think of it as a universal truth. You can't refute it. I've tried.

Start investing *now* and you can retire wealthy. That's the magic of investing. Compound interest is *magic*. It's not really magic, it's very logical. But it's *fun*!

To quote a dear friend, "Money is math." I've learned math *can* be fun when it's understood, when it has to do with money, and especially when you get to watch it grow.

Exponentially.

Please pay yourself first.

Do you have as much fun as I do running retirement/investment scenarios through those online calculators? Do you know the difference between financial freedom and financial independence?

LIFE IS MESSY.

Life tosses curve balls. Life is never exactly according to plan, if we even have a plan.

There's so much fun that can be had outside the lines. I've had some of my most amazing opportunities to learn and grow and be and do that were *only* possible because life got messy.

Life is messy *and* beautiful.

When life feels messy, make the most of it. Learn to let go of control. Control is only an illusion anyway.

Embrace the wildness and the wonder that comes into our lives when we least expect it.

Take that new path.

Love in ways you were not expecting.

Embrace yourself for exactly who you are in every moment.

Love others for their messiness. Don't judge.

Only love.

Even through the messes.

I like to think of the silver linings. Because there are *always* silver linings.

How did it feel the last time life got messy? What were the silver linings?

You always have a choice. Always.

No matter what the situation is, there is always a choice. The choice could be action you can choose to take (or not take), or a shift in perspective. Or both.

You are not a victim.

Create healthy boundaries. If someone is treating you badly, leave. Staying is a choice. If you have a situation you can't leave you can always choose to change your perspective.

What will your perspective be?

Shitty things are going to happen. That's when perspective matters most. It doesn't mean you won't be in pain. It doesn't mean you won't grieve. All it means is you can choose how you will look at it. It might mean getting professional help. Confiding in loved ones. Talking things through.

Whatever it takes, your perspective can change your life, for good or bad.

Remembering this can make all the difference. I promise.

Is there anything you're walking through today that could benefit from making a different choice? Is there something happening that makes you feel like you have no choices?

FORGIVENESS IS NOT ABOUT THEM. IT'S A GIFT YOU GIVE YOURSELF.

I've wasted so much time waiting on someone to come asking for forgiveness. No one in particular. Just anyone who'd ever pissed me off.

Then I learned something incredibly powerful. Forgiveness is *not* something you do for *them*; forgiveness is something you do for *you*.

It's a gift. It's priceless. I'm a firm believer that if I live a life forgiving others, I'll live a longer life. Worst case, at least it'll be a much happier life!

You'll get hurt. You might be betrayed. By people who might never know how they've made you feel. Even if they know, they might not think, or choose, to ask you for forgiveness.

Them asking for forgiveness is irrelevant to whether it's in your best interest to grant it.

What matters is your choice to forgive.

Forgiving someone *doesn't* mean you're ok with that thing they did that needed forgiving, or that you'll want them to stay in your life. Forgiveness *does* mean you value your peace, and you're honoring your boundaries, you're not letting another human steal your precious energy, time or headspace.

Forgive.

Then choose the space you're willing to give them in your life. Or not. But please forgive.

Is there anyone who has harmed you that you'd like to forgive, even if they haven't asked for forgiveness? Is there something you've had to forgive me for that I haven't acknowledged?

Pay your taxes. On time. Or early.

I was never taught about money, finances, personal responsibility, or financial accountability. It's been a hard lesson to learn, and it's involved moving through fear, learning to live within my means, doing the paperwork, making the calls, and ultimately owning it.

I know I wasn't the role model for you financially, which is why I want to own it now, admit it to you, and say "Please pay your taxes."

It's a privilege to live in a place that, for the most part, gives us what we need when we need it.

It's so much easier to keep up with taxes from the beginning. If you have a paycheck, make sure your deductions work for you. If you're self-employed, be responsible for filing and paying 100% of your own taxes. Or hire someone to do it for you.

Whatever it takes to not only get it done but get it done right.

Now I look forward to filing, getting it done early and on my own.

Maybe that's weird.

But it feels so good.

Do you like to prepare and file your own taxes, or hire someone to do it for you? Do you file on time?

No one has all their shit together all the time.

No matter what anyone says, no one has it all together. The ones who seem the most put together can sometimes be so, umm, *not*.

What I want to say here isn't about anyone else though. Life is beautiful and messy, and it's often the messes that make us more beautiful.

Be real. Be yourself.

Never judge yourself by what you *think* others are doing, or thinking, or putting on social media.

Own your mistakes. Own your mess.

The humans I love most are often the ones who own their shit, walk through fire and come out the other side a bit better for making the most of the lessons learned.

You'll have moments where you feel like you have it all together! And you will. And then you won't. And then you will.

Just like everyone else.

Is it hard to remember that the ones that look like they have it all going on, don't always have it all going on? Do you feel pressure to look like you always have it all together?

Vulnerability is strength, not weakness.

I have felt the happiest, the strongest, the most alive, the freest, when I've been the most vulnerable. There is strength in vulnerability. There's no hiding. There are no lies. You're exactly who you are in those moments. They can be scary and intimidating. Vulnerability can feel like a free-fall.

Vulnerability in...

love.

friendship.

asking for help.

putting yourself out there.

doing that thing.

walking toward.

walking away.

For me it's like knowing I have so much to lose and yet honoring what it is I know I need or want at my soul level. Saying that thing. Asking for what's important. Setting that boundary. Asking for help. Letting someone see the darkest parts of me, because I also trust them to see the light in me.

If I lose something because I allowed myself to be vulnerable it probably wasn't meant for me anyway.

Do you lean into, or away from, moments where you might feel vulnerable? What parts of life can make you feel the most vulnerable?

SOCIAL MEDIA IS A MIND-FUCK.

I'm sure you already know this. It's the perfect storm when you feel less than; when you're lonely; having a bad day.

Walking through a breakup.

Even on a good day it can mess with your head.

Always remember no one puts their worst out there for the world to see. It's always the right pose. The right filter. The right words.

We all do it.

It's fun.

It's creative.

It's also only the parts of us we want people to see.

Speaking of social media, please don't use it to stalk anyone. Your exes. Your crush. Your ex's new girlfriend.

You can *always* find the thing that tells you you're the wrong size, shape, color, height, even the wrong person.

If you're looking for it, you'll find it.

Also, just because he watches your stories or comments on your posts does *not* mean you should go back to him.

Feel free to block.

It's not personal. And it can go both ways.

I promise.

Have you ever hidden, blocked, or unfollowed a social media account because of how it made you feel? How does it feel when you see someone putting their truth out there for all to see even when it's messy?

LET GO OF JUDGMENT.

Don't judge yourself.

Then you can begin to stop judging others.

I was only able to stop judging others when I stopped judging myself. I didn't realize I'd grown up judging myself constantly. I came by it honestly.

I thought all women were judging me, and each other. Which was a judgment of *them*.

The irony is not lost on me.

When I could learn to stop judging myself it was amazing to see how easy it was to also not judge others, *especially* women.

My inner peace grew. I was a better friend, sister, mother, partner, co-worker. Even a better stranger!

I liked everyone more.

I love that when I change the way I look at things, the things I look at change.

Funny how that works.

Do you feel like you're hard on yourself or others, even just in your thoughts? Do you ever struggle with feeling judged when no one is saying or doing anything judgmental toward you?

_____
_____
_____
_____
_____
_____
_____
_____
_____
_____
_____
_____
_____
_____
_____
_____
_____
_____
_____
_____
_____
_____
_____
_____
_____
_____
_____
_____

You are not your thoughts.

Your head can be a scary place to spend your time. I know, because mine is. There's not a single human who doesn't have thoughts that are better left unsaid.

Desires better left dormant.

Paths better not taken.

They say your first thought is not your responsibility, but your second thought is.

Well, sometimes it'll be your second through ninth, or maybe even 27th.

And that's ok.

Because what counts is what you do with them. Or not.

I do know that what I let myself dwell on is where I end up.

Thoughts will become things.

Take care of your space.

Your headspace.

Declutter often, and well.

What's a thought that became a thing for you, that maybe you wish hadn't? What do you do when you're having those second, third, fourth... twenty-fifth thoughts that you know aren't that great for your headspace?

EXPECTATION IS THE ROOT OF RESENTMENT.

I don't mean we don't expect people to be good and kind. And this isn't talking about boundaries.

I'm talking about expectations that are based on what we *think* we need someone to do so that we feel ok.

This can be a boyfriend, lover, coworker, client, friend. Anyone really. Your mom, for example.

Unmet expectations will fester. It's a universal law. There's no avoiding it.

You'll get a resentment toward that person.

Your relationship will suffer.

If you think someone should (or shouldn't) be doing something, then have a conversation. It's really that simple.

You get to let them know how you feel and why it's important to you.

They get to listen and let you know how they feel about it.

Then they get to choose.

That's right. They get to decide what they will (or won't) do.

Then you get to choose.

Choose wisely.

By the way, I really, really dislike the word should. Because, well, 'should' – according to whom?

Just so you know.

Do you have an unrealistic expectation about someone right now? If you do, can you let it go? Or have the conversation?

YOUR HEAD IS YOUR BIGGEST COMPETITOR.

Your head and heart have kept you alive this long and they want to keep doing it. They want to keep you safe. So that you don't die.

Whenever you're ready to do that thing, to break the mold, to take that chance, your head and heart will often do everything they can to keep you alive. To keep you safe.

Just like if you're on the plains of Africa about to trek out alone. Into the night. Which means you could possibly get eaten by lions. Your body will react and go into survival mode.

It doesn't matter that you're only about to skydive for the first time. Or go on that interview. Or start that business.

You'll get all sorts of crazy thoughts like 'who am I to do this thing', 'to be this person'.

Your head is your biggest competition.

Absolutely no one else is thinking anything remotely that unkind, that discouraging.

Take back the conversation as if you were talking to a beautiful girlfriend who wanted to do that thing, to be that person.

And then do that thing anyway.

Because walking through fear is growth.

Fear always comes before growth.

Remember that.

What does survival mode physically feel like in your body? What does your head tell you? What can you do to take back the story?

AVOID MANIPULATION.

We all want to get what we want. It's human. The more we want something the easier it can be to fall into manipulating someone to get it.

It's not worth it and it never feels good.

I spent so much of my life perfecting the ability to manipulate.

I remember someone I loved calling me out on it – 'you're a manipulator just like your mother'. I don't know which stung more. The fact he called me a manipulator or compared me to my mom.

He was right, but I wasn't ready to hear it yet. It took me about five more years and lots of pain to finally hear the truth in his words. Words I'd not forgotten.

Manipulation can look like many different things. It can be hurtful passive aggressive behavior (silent treatment, withdrawing affection). It can also look like things that feel good (gifts, physical affection, beautiful words).

Getting something because of successful manipulation will never feel as good as getting something that someone truly was moved to give because they just wanted to.

You'll respect them more for it.

More importantly, you'll respect yourself.

Even when the answer is no.

Have you ever knowingly manipulated a person or situation to get what you wanted? How did it feel?

Your 40s will blow your mind.

In my 20s I thought I had it going on.

In my 30s I thought I knew everything.

In my 40s I realized I had so much to learn and that I was seriously far from having my shit together. That realization made my life so much better!

It was such freedom. Mental liberation of ridiculous preconceived ideas I had about who and what I should be.

In my 40s I learned to love myself. I learned to love my body. Which also allowed me to be able to have the best sex of my life. Not because of anyone else, but because of me.

I promise that when you feel that way about yourself, about your body, your partner will reflect that admiration back at you.

Own your body.

Own your curves.

Own every single mark, scar, freckle, and line.

They are the story of you.

When you embrace you, you can't help but become a bright attractive light of love and adventure.

People in your life respond.

It's a beautiful thing.

Do you believe you have lots to learn, room to grow, perspectives to change? How does that make you feel?

GOOD BOOTS ARE ESSENTIAL.

You can wear boots anytime and with anything.

Or nothing. Because that's sexy too.

My favorite boots took me all over England on my first solo trip overseas.

Put miles and miles on your favorite boots.

Play with them.

Wear tall ones in the bedroom with knee socks.

Cowboy boots with a hat.

He'll like it.

Have you invested in an amazing pair of boots? Where are some of the places they're going to take you?

4

THE BIG PICTURE

LIFE IS HOW YOU SPEND YOUR DASH. There's an amazing poem called The Dash, written by Linda Ellis. The dash is referring to that little hyphen that separates someone's year of birth from their year of death. That space between.

What will you do with the time you have? The moments. The spaces. The unknown. I know that I am who I am at this moment because of the life I've had. All of it. The things I've done, as well as the things I haven't done. I love all of it and the person I am today.

Do I have regrets? Yeah. Have I hurt others deeply? Yes. I wish with all my being that I had never hurt anyone. But that is an impossibility. You'll have regrets, you'll cause hurt, you'll do amazing things, you'll wish you'd done things you hadn't.

What I just hope you believe is that you can do or be anything your heart desires. Here are some things I wish I'd known sooner.

xo – Mom

"Life is what happens when you're busy making other plans." – John Lennon

THERE IS NOTHING YOU CANNOT DO, IF YOU WRITE IT DOWN.

It's taken me a long time to figure this one out. This book I'm writing to you is one of the results of my figuring it out. At 53.

If a goal isn't written down, it's only a good idea.

Hold on to that idea, and it'll serve you well.

Put goals on sticky notes.

Write them on the mirror.

Keep a notebook on you.

Put them in your phone.

Put them on a vision board.

I'm old school so I like to see them in front of me. Putting them somewhere virtually is better than nothing as far as I'm concerned but putting them on paper is so incredibly powerful!

And if you can write it out by hand, there's something about the pen to paper connection that activates your subconscious in ways that putting it into your phone just can't touch.

What are a few goals you have that you'd like to write down somewhere? What's one goal you reached that you know for a fact was only achieved because you'd written it down?

IT NEVER HURTS TO ASK.

You get what you ask for. You also *don't* get what you *don't* ask for. Most of the time anyway. So, figure out what you want and just ask.

If the answer is no, well, nothing lost, nothing gained.

You really have nothing to lose.

Ask for that raise.

Ask me anything you want.

Ask yourself why.

Ask for help.

Ask them how.

Ask that guy for his number.

Ask yourself why not.

Just ask.

What are a couple things you'd like to ask for? What are some of the best things you've gotten only because you asked for them?

It's never too late.

I remember when I realized that if I changed my career path in my 40s, I could ultimately spend more time in my new career than my old one.

It's never too late to do or try or be anything your heart desires.

Until it is.

Please promise me you'll listen to your heart's desires and give each one some serious thought before ever writing anything off.

What adventures do you want to have?

What hobbies do you want to learn?

Who do you want to love?

What do you want to put out in the world?

Today, tomorrow, someday.

Listen to your heart and soul.

And then be, do, feel, see, learn, love whatever it is that is most important to you.

What's one of your heart's desires? What can you do to make it happen?

You *will* fall. You *will* fail. Please just get back up.

Your failures are where you'll become the best possible version of you. I'm a big advocate of failing because it's in failing that I've learned to grow and change.

Can we really call it failing though? Maybe failing is just another way of learning.

Remember the wise words of Thomas Edison who said he didn't fail, he just found 10,000 ways that wouldn't work.

If I let failure hold me back, I would've missed out on great love, on work I'm passionate about, on new ventures.

The only true failure is in not getting back up.

Always, always just get back up.

What are some things you've failed at? How has it made you feel? What have you learned from failing?

DON'T LET FEAR HOLD YOU BACK.

Some of my very first memories are fear-based.

The large black centipede in my crib, my mom's loud and sudden reaction, yanking me up out of my crib.

The earthquake in the middle of the night. Again, being yanked up and out of my crib by my mom who stood in the bedroom doorway with me in her arms.

The local drugstore's gently sloping ramp that I just couldn't bring myself to walk down. I remember standing there, about 4 years old, frozen in terror at the thought of navigating those 15 feet or so of carpeted sloping expanse.

As an adult I've been paralyzed at the thought of life changes. The end of relationships, long or short, didn't matter. Fear of being alone.

Financial fears.

Fear of what others might think.

Walk through your fear. Identify it, feel it, honor it, and then do that thing.

I've jumped out of a plane at 13,000'. Started businesses. Published my deepest thoughts and darkest feelings. Fallen in love. Walked away from things that were hurtful to me.

Walked into the unknown.

By doing those things I've discovered some of the most powerful and interesting parts of myself.

You can do it. You can do anything.

I believe in you. I always have.

You are strong. You are brave. You are safe.

What's one of your biggest fears? How can you navigate through it?

5

SEX

MAGICAL. SACRED. INTIMATE. Sex is the most powerful creative energy there is. It's in your core. It's a gift. It's gold. Spend it wisely.

I'd give anything to have been able to openly talk about sex with my mom. I hope you feel you can talk to me about it. Any of it.

xo – Mom

"When it comes to sex, the most important six inches are the ones between the ears." – Dr. Ruth

Sex changes everything.

It does. I'm sure you already know this. Sometimes I wonder about your first time.

How it made you feel, as a woman.

No matter how old you are or who you're having sex with, it *will* change things.

It's an inescapable biological fact. Bonding chemicals are released. Your feelings will be affected, with or without an orgasm.

I promise you.

Please remember this when you choose to have sex with someone.

Will you truly be ok if you are not with this person again?

Can you imagine being ok if they're having sex with other people?

If there's no talk of exclusivity, please assume you're not exclusive.

Just be sure you're ok with that.

Because sex changes everything.

*What are some of the feelings that get stirred up in you after you have sex?
Do you honor them or is it easier to just try to ignore them?*

SEX IS BEAUTIFUL.

Always believe that sex is beautiful. I haven't always felt that way.

There were times I gave it away for all the wrong reasons. I was lonely. I needed touch. I didn't want to lose someone. I didn't want another person to have my partner, not because I loved him, but because being with him made me feel better about myself.

I got to a place that made me wonder if sex could ever be beautiful again.

Had I crossed a line? A line in my heart and soul. My body.

I was not being true to myself. And that has always had the power to make me feel shame.

Could sex ever be special again?

Yes! It's special again.

Sex *is* beautiful. It never stopped being beautiful, I had only stopped treating it like the sacred thing it is.

If you ever feel like sex isn't special, maybe take a break. Look inside. Let go of any shame you might be holding. Know that living your truth will bring it all back around for you.

I promise.

Because sex is beautiful.

Do you believe that sex is a beautiful magical experience? Has it ever lost its specialness for you?

Sᴇx ᴄᴀɴ ʙᴇ ᴀᴍᴀᴢɪɴɢ ᴀɴᴅ sɪʟʟʏ ᴀᴛ ᴛʜᴇ sᴀᴍᴇ ᴛɪᴍᴇ.

Some of the best sex ends up in giggles. In belly laughs. I love that.

Don't ever take yourself, or your partner, too seriously.

Play.

Tease.

Bodies make noises.

Bodies do things.

Bodies don't do things.

Do you feel free to be silly during sex? What's the funniest thing that's happened to you and your partner during sex?

CHEMISTRY IS NOT LOVE.

I'm a romantic at heart. I believe in the *feeling* of love at first sight. That's that thing called chemistry.

Chemistry is a great trickster, but it's oh so fun!

I've been fooled by chemistry more than once and the irony is that I can't even remember who they were.

I hope you experience all of it. Love at first sight. Incredible chemistry. True love. But always remember that chemistry is *not* an indicator of compatibility. Especially early chemistry, that butterflies in the belly feeling. That heart-pounding effect someone we hardly know can have on us.

I'm sure you know this feeling.

It's beautiful, exciting, enthralling, intriguing.

It can also lead to heartbreak.

It can make you do things you might later wish you hadn't.

If I could sum it up in a sentence, this would be it:

Be cautious with chemistry.

Have you ever experienced love at first sight? Did it grow into a real love?

SAY *YES*. SAY *NO*. MEAN WHAT YOU SAY.

You have the right to choose anything you do or don't want to do at any time when it involves your body. It doesn't matter if it's something you've done before, you can still say *No*.

Don't ever be afraid to say *No* with strength and intention.

Know that even if it's not easy to say, or you're feeling weak in the moment, it doesn't matter.

If you say *No*, your *No* must be respected.

Saying *Yes* is just as important. Say it with conviction and mean it.

Please don't ever say *Yes* unless you wholeheartedly mean it. If you're unsure whether you want to say *Yes* or *No*, please say *No*. Until you are sure you want to say *Yes*.

A real man will listen to you, every time.

A real man will wait for you.

Have you ever wanted to say No but didn't? Have you ever said Yes and then regretted it? How have those times made you feel?

TELL HIM WHAT YOU LIKE. TELL HIM WHAT YOU DON'T LIKE.

I couldn't do this until I was in my 40s. Which was about 20 years too late. I didn't even know my own body. I had never thought there might be more to know, to explore, to feel.

It's a powerful thing when a woman knows her body, what she likes, what she doesn't like, *and is able to tell her partner*. It's not easy to get there.

Do you know what you like? What you don't? Explore. Explore your body, explore it alone, explore it with a partner.

This is about so much more than just sex.

It can be about all the senses.

Touch. Taste. Sound. Speed. Visuals.

Own your pleasure.

Telling your partner what you want can be very erotic. Hearing you verbalize your desires, feeling you guide their hands, their body. Discovering your secret places.

In your body, your mind, your heart, your soul.

It's empowering. It's also vulnerable as fuck.

It'll be good for you. And him.

Make it about *what you like*, instead of *what he isn't doing*. He might think you're not happy with what he's doing. How you say it makes all the difference.

If he doesn't want to hear what you want to say, remember that part isn't about you.

Do you know what you do like and what you don't like? Are you comfortable letting your partner know?

BE SAFE.

Always have the STD talk *before* you decide to have sex. Here are some facts:

Herpes is contagious and can be spread even if the person has not had any signs or symptoms.

Most people don't know they have it because it's not part of the standard 'please run an STD test on me' blood panel.

When someone gets an all-clear from a standard STD check they *have not* been tested for either oral herpes (HSV-1) or genital herpes (HSV-2).

Just be safe. Use condoms until you know you're both clear, and until you're both in agreement that you're in a monogamous relationship.

I will tell you that most men do not want to use condoms, even when they find out a partner has herpes.

Many other STDs can be easily cured with antibiotics. If you have unprotected sex, please just go get tested and specifically ask them to test for HSV-1 and HSV-2. They will likely tell you that they only test for those if you have symptoms. Tell them you still want to be tested, and a good doctor will honor your request and write it up.

STDs are not shameful. But they can be dangerous.

Please, be safe.

Do you always have the STD talk before you have sex with a new partner? Have you ever asked to be tested for both oral and genital herpes?

6

LOVE

LOVE HARD & WITH ALL YOU HAVE. Love isn't easy, and it isn't always fun or exciting or passionate. But it's always worth it. No matter what. I've loved a few times in my life and I know I'll love again. Some loves have come and gone. Some loves have stayed and will forever occupy a place in my heart and soul. Even when I do love again.

Love can be scary and might make you feel like running the other direction. Please give it a chance at least once in your life. Stay with it. Let it grow. Let it hurt. Let it be. Love can be exciting and intoxicating and make you want to dive in headfirst, imagining the rest of your life with this person. It can make you do crazy things, or at least things other people might call crazy. I've done the running and I've done the diving. Neither is wrong. And both can lead to amazing things.

xo – Mom

"LOVE HAS NOTHING TO DO WITH WHAT YOU ARE EXPECTING TO GET – only with what you are expecting to give – which is everything." – Katherine Hepburn

FOLLOW YOUR HEART.

Love anyone you want. Don't ever let another human tell you who you should or shouldn't love.

Don't let your head tell you who you should or shouldn't love.

Staying with someone when your heart's not in it can be selfish. Everyone deserves to be loved fully and completely and if your heart isn't in it, you'll know. So will they.

Do both of you a favor and figure it out.

Do you love them?

Do you truly want to stay? If you want to stay, figure it out and do the work.

Don't stay just because you're afraid to leave.

Follow your heart.

Have you ever stayed with someone because you were afraid to leave? Have you ever regretted following your heart?

LOVE BIG. LOVE HARD.

Letting another person into my heart, letting myself fall in love has felt like standing on the edge of a deep, dark precipice. It's also been the best feeling in the world when I'm in it.

A chemical rush is unavoidable, but that feeling isn't a predictor of real love. It's all the rest of it that has shaped me.

Letting myself walk through the inevitable ups and downs of truly loving another human, feeling the ecstasy, the comfort, the companionship, the heartbreak, the freedom, the pain, the beauty, the frustration, and all the other feelings I haven't been able to put into words.

Those are the things that have made me love. It's building a connection with another human. Knowing their heart and soul and letting them know mine.

All the places. Even the ugly ones. Don't be afraid, my love.

You will fall. You will break.

You will soar. You will love.

Just let it in. You'll know what I mean.

Don't be afraid to love big. Don't be afraid to love hard.

How would you describe love when you're in it? How does love make you feel?

Love unconditionally.

I believe that the only way to say I truly love someone is to love them unconditionally. To me, loving someone unconditionally doesn't mean they can do whatever they want without consequences to my feelings or our relationship.

Loving unconditionally means that I'll love him no matter what he might do. Because I love him.

It's his actions that will tell me how he feels, about me, about us, about himself. Then I get to choose. If he somehow breaks my heart, I get to choose. Will I stay? Will I go?

Loving unconditionally does *not* mean I'm willing to tolerate bad behavior.

It means that there are no strings attached to my love.

It doesn't mean I don't have boundaries.

It means I want him to be who he is. That is the man I love. If he turns out to be not who I thought he was, my feelings might change.

I might fall out of love. Feelings changing doesn't mean the love was conditional.

I can *love* unconditionally, and yet *be* with him conditionally.

That's the difference. To me.

How do you feel about the idea of unconditional love? Do you relate more to the idea of conditional or unconditional love for a partner?

THE OPPOSITE OF LOVE IS INDIFFERENCE.

Indifference is a very hard feeling for me to sit with when it's coming my way from someone I care about.

For so much of my life, I would have chosen to feel them hating me. It's that feeling of him being so angry, so done, so upset with me. At least then I'd feel I still meant something to him.

I've also been on the other end of this.

I've been the hateful, hurtful, angry one. I realized it was because I still had feelings. They might be feelings of hurt and upset, but they were still rooted in love and passion.

But it was when I no longer cared what happened, or felt their actions had no effect on me that I knew I was no longer *in love* with them.

I was indifferent. Not detached, just no longer invested in any outcome.

Indifference is the opposite of love.

How would you describe the feeling of realizing you're no longer in love with someone? Have you ever felt anything you'd describe as indifference?

Respect is key.

I remember the moment I realized I must *respect* a man to love him. My best friend and I were having a picnic in our favorite park while trying to figure out what it took for each of us to truly feel we could love a man.

After a few hours it hit me. If I lost respect for the man I was with, my love would fade away and there was no getting it back.

It made everything about my past relationships make sense. I looked at my loves and realized the times my feelings faded inexplicably were because I had lost respect.

It was having already respected and loved him and then something would happen that eroded my respect for him. It could be something he did, or didn't, do.

Yeah, maybe they were things I came to expect or want from him, which isn't fair to him. But those expectations still affected my respect. (It took me years to learn how damaging expectations are.)

I'd only realized in hindsight, I must respect a man, especially if I'd like to fall, and stay, in love with him.

Understanding this made me look at how I loved and respected myself. Could I say I truly loved myself if I was doing things that didn't show respect to myself?

Respect yourself. Then love yourself. Then respect him. Then love him. I believe that's how it works, that they are *all* intertwined. I know they are, for me.

How important is it to you to respect your partner? Have you ever lost respect for someone you love?

TAKE YOUR TIME.

There's never a need to rush love. Love takes time to grow.

I've been convinced it was love, and then realized in hindsight that it was lust. Or a crush. Or I had just wanted to be in love so badly that I'd call anything love.

If it's the right person, they'll give you space to take your time.

You don't *have to* take your time. But you also don't have to be afraid you'll lose them if you do.

Because if you lose them because you took your time, well then, they weren't the person for you anyway.

Have you ever rushed into love? Have you ever taken your time falling in love?

Unrequited love is not romantic.

Why would you want to be with someone who isn't choosing you?

Why would you pine for someone who's moved on?

Why would you choose to let someone hold space in your heart when they haven't earned it?

Unrequited love, in my opinion, is an excuse to be unavailable for real love.

I've been there. I idealized a man who had made his choice clear. I believed that he'd figure it out and come back to me.

One day it hit me square in the face. Why would I so desperately want to be with someone who doesn't want to be with me?

Why would I give sweet space in my heart to someone who isn't returning my love?

It took a long time to figure that one out. But finally, my heart is happy and free.

It was never about him. I had to learn to become available for someone willing to love.

Unrequited love was a great excuse to stay aloof.

Unrequited love was my way of avoiding feelings.

There is nothing romantic about unrequited love.

Have you ever idealized unrequited love? Have you ever experienced it?

7

HIM

THERE IS NOTHING LIKE THE LOVE OF A GOOD MAN. In my opinion. And contrary to popular opinion, good men are *not* hard to find. I hope you choose wisely, with your heart *and* your head. Someday you might want to find him; you might want to share your life with him. Or maybe not. There is no should. I only want you to be happy and content.

If your future does involve a man, here's a collection of some of my favorite concepts around the whole man thing. Even remembering a few of them has the potential to save years of heartbreak. I promise. Because these are all things I've either felt or done myself.

If someone had told me these not-so-secret secrets, I could've avoided so much pain. But my path has made me who I am today. I hope you can learn from my experience. Even though I know you'll make your own path.

xo – Mom

"After a while you just want to be with the one who makes you laugh." – Mr. Big (Sex And The City)

It's not his job to take care of your feelings.

I remember the first time I heard this one. I was in my 40s and heartbroken. I wanted to tell him how I felt. I was blubbering to a woman who felt like my own mother, a woman I loved and respected.

She said, "It's not his job to take care of your feelings."

I'd never ever heard anyone say that. I believed that of course the man I was with needs to know and understand what I'm feeling and then make me feel better. I believed he needed to do whatever it took to make me ok.

Not only did her words smack me upside the head, she also basically told me that it's not his job to listen to all my feelings about whatever it was I was feeling. She reminded me that's what girlfriends and therapists are for.

Your feelings are your own responsibility. He better treat you well and not intentionally hurt your feelings, but your actual feelings are *not* his responsibility.

This was a mic drop moment for me. I hope it is for you.

Have you ever felt it's your partner's job to make you feel ok? Do you feel like you have healthy boundaries around how much you share your feelings with your partner?

No answer is an answer.
    Silence is an answer.
    Maybe means no.
    The only thing that means yes is yes.
    He isn't in the hospital.
    He isn't dead.
    He didn't lose your number.
    If a man can't figure out how to contact you in this day and age, well let's just say I hope he's not the one you're interested in.

Can you let go of something, or someone, when you don't get an answer? Or when you don't get the answer you want?

A GOOD MAN WILL BE CONSISTENT.
    A man who *deserves* your heart will be consistent.
    You won't wonder if he wants to see you.
    You'll know exactly where you stand with him.
    He'll show up.
    A man that isn't consistent with you is just *not that into you*.
    A quality man won't leave you wondering.
    You'll know.
    Because he'll be consistent.

Do you require a partner to be consistent? Is it easy for you to let go of someone who isn't consistent?

IT'S NOT ABOUT *HIM* CHOOSING *YOU*.

I wish I had known this as a girl. As a young woman. I always felt like it was about getting *him* to choose *me*.

Whoever *he* was.

That is *not* how it's supposed to work.

Please only choose him because you *want* to choose him, and not just because he is choosing you.

Have you always felt like you've chosen your partner? Have you ever felt like you've wanted to get someone who isn't actively choosing you to choose you?

DON'T TRY TO MAKE HIM JEALOUS.

Doing something with the intention of making your man jealous will always backfire. It won't make you feel good. If you ever begin to head down the path of wanting to make him jealous, take a good look at where you're both at.

Ask yourself why you're feeling this way, why you'd want to cause him pain.

Do you feel unloved? Do you feel like he's ignoring you? Is *he* doing something causing *you* to feel jealous?

Well, it could be any of these reasons or a million others. What I'm getting at is this; if you feel the desire to actively create jealousy there's a bigger problem that needs to be addressed.

Jealousy will *never* improve a relationship. Please don't try to make him jealous.

Sort out your feelings around why you might want to do this, and then take action to change your perspective.

Is there something you need to communicate to him about his actions? Is there an insecurity within you that you recognize you've had even before he came into your life?

Creating jealousy is never a good idea.

Have you ever wanted to make your partner jealous? If you ever feel like this, what's something you could do about it, that could improve your relationship?

Just say hi. And smile.

The power of a smile is priceless. Especially your smile, because you are beautiful!

Smile at him. Them. Everyone.

When you're open and friendly, the universe responds in kind.

Others will be open and friendly with you.

It just takes that one person.

That person you notice.

The one who makes you a slight bit scared to say hi.

Yes, that one.

Just say hi, and smile.

It works.

Have you ever done this? Is this something you can easily do?

He's just not that into you.

If you have to wonder if he's into you you have your answer. Please don't linger. Don't wait for him to figure it out.

Don't fall in love with him

Don't chase him.

A man who is into you will make sure you never have to ask yourself this question.

If he wants to talk to you, he'll call.

If he wants to see you, he'll arrange a date.

If he wants to text you, you'll get a text.

If he isn't doing these things, he's just not that into you.

And that's ok.

Move on.

This is one of those that took me way too long to figure out for myself. I hope that you can hold your head high and just move on. Because you're worth it.

Have you ever held on to the idea of someone too long, hoping they'd finally figure it out and show up for you? How do you feel when this happens to you? Is it easy for you to let go and move on?

Let him go.

If he chooses to leave, let him go. If you're meant to be together, he'll come back.

I promise.

This has been one of the most freeing actions I've ever learned to take when a relationship ends. Even if I didn't want it to be over.

I learned this from that wise woman, the one who taught me that it's not his job to take care of my feelings.

She also told me that if two are meant to be there is nothing that will keep them from coming back together, no matter how long they might be apart.

I promise you that it works.

Have you ever let someone truly go and then had them come back? Have you ever come back to someone after they let you go?

THERE WILL ALWAYS BE MORE TO LEARN, FEEL, LOVE, LOSE, GAIN AND through it all you're going to be okay.

My beautiful daughter, this is my last page written specifically to you. There is still so much I want to say to you.

Please let's talk more, talk often and talk deeply. It won't always be easy but know that I'll be trying my best to understand you always.

When I say things that are hurtful (because I'm sure I will) please know it is never my intention to cause you any pain with my words.

Please let me know if my words are ever hurtful.

You have the rest of your life ahead of you and I can't wait to see all the amazingness you have headed your way.

I believe with all my heart you are resilient, you are good, you are kind, you are smart, you are beautiful, you are generous, you are compassionate.

Please always believe this and always be true to yourself.

I have always loved you and I always will.

xo – Mom

Would you like to talk? I would love to.

ABOUT THE AUTHOR

PATRICE ROSSI – Author, speaker, creator, coach, daughter, sister, mother-of-boys, ex-wife, ex-girlfriend, friend, avid traveler, photographer; all the things.

Things I'd Tell My Daughter is written from the heart with touches of irreverence, based on her experiences growing up and her attempts at adulting the best she can; a compilation of musings she wishes her own mother had been able to share with her.

Things I'd Tell My Daughter is written to the daughter she doesn't have, the daughter she is, and all daughters everywhere.

www.ingramcontent.com/pod-product-compliance
Lightning Source LLC
Chambersburg PA
CBHW070633030426
42337CB00020B/3994